Muddy Matterhorn

Also by Heather McHugh

Poems
Feeler (chapbook)
Upgraded to Serious
Eyeshot
The Father of the Predicaments
Hinge & Sign: Poems, 1968–1993
Shades
To the Quick
A World of Difference
Dangers

Prose
Broken English: Poetry and Partiality

Translations
Cyclops (by Euripides)
Glottal Stop: 101 Poems by Paul Celan (with Nikolai Popov)
Because the Sea Is Black: Poems of Blaga Dimitrova (with Nikolai Popov)
D'Après Tout: Poems by Jean Follain

Anthology
The Best American Poetry 2007 (with David Lehman)

Muddy Matterhorn
Poems 2009–2019
Heather McHugh

Copper Canyon Press
Port Townsend, Washington

Cover art: Robert Richarz

Copper Canyon Press is in residence at Fort Worden State Park in Port Townsend, Washington, under the auspices of Centrum. Centrum is a gathering place for artists and creative thinkers from around the world, students of all ages and backgrounds, and audiences seeking extraordinary cultural enrichment.

LIBRARY OF CONGRESS CATALOGING-IN-PUBLICATION DATA
Names: McHugh, Heather, 1948– author.
Title: Muddy matterhorn : poems 2009–2019 / Heather McHugh.
Description: Port Townsend, Washington : Copper Canyon Press, [2020]
Identifiers: LCCN 2019043664 | ISBN 9781556595967 (trade paperback)
Subjects: LCGFT: Poetry.
Classification: LCC PS3563.A311614 M83 2020 | DDC 811/.54—dc23
LC record available at https://lccn.loc.gov/2019043664

98765432 FIRST PRINTING

COPPER CANYON PRESS
Post Office Box 271
Port Townsend, Washington 98368
www.coppercanyonpress.org

Acknowledgments

Ten years on: divorce, retirement, several moves, a house fire in a snow-storm, losses among friends—and now I'm on the upper side of seventy. Apologies to anyone, for anything I've missed. Happy to update my files, if you refresh my memory bank.

Poems here appeared in literary journals such as *Free Verse, Grist, Gianthology, The Malahat Review, Scoundrel Time,* and *The Sewanee Review*. Half the poems formed the 2019 chapbook *Feeler* (Sarabande); I thank you, Sarah Gorham and Michael Wiegers, for making possible the overlap.

I owe Frizzelle and Shields, my writer friends, for their encourage-ments, early and late; and John Pierce for uncommon gifts of patience. As a lifesaving literary-textual adviser for the likes of me (who bring gram-matical precisions to my grounds but poetical rebellions to my airs), reader David Caligiuri has no peer. He ruined me for others.

Saboteur, by opening a world-class bakery in Bremerton, kept me stocked in happy paradox (high art, low church). Port Angeles's Blackbird Coffeehouse afforded other welcomes in its turn—my weakness was a yodeler's fanfare of Swiss butterhorns.

Speaking of bread, how not to mention the MacArthur folks? Their material faith in my instincts helped me do more than a few good works during the decade following the brouhaha of that award. From 2011 to 2018, I learned a lot (as politics itself should do) from those we channeled respite to—the long-term caregivers of others who, by birth or fate, were incapacitated. I didn't stand alone to honor them: a hundred soul mates rose to the occasion, too; and all of them deserve high fives.

The best in human company: Let me ignite a line of Roman candles here, to celebrate my man. This book saw light because of him. The care it took to write, I took for him. On entering or exiting a dinghy, I'm every bit as graceful as a turtle. But I leap into some other crafts half-decently. I here resort to those, the better to be seen and heard:

This book's a toast to Rich, above all Rich: his questionable humor, answerable heart, and master hand. (O lord, there are no words.)

Contents

Muddy Matterhorn

Indivisible by Dark

I

I wrote the a.
Then x'd it out.
I'd 24 more characters
to doubt. I traced them black,
erased them red. By then I was

undone by zed.

II

The numbers followed, one by one,
and two by four, and more
by ninety-three—

I numbered every being I'd begun
till numbers wanted numbing rights to me.

III

Perhaps there were no more of
any one. No group to grab,
no times to table, and no saming
to a name. I'd only oddities.

I saw remark was marking's own
duplicity; I saw that zero

owed its all to one.
When we fell silent,

it was quotably.

IV

Now none
was insignificant.

I wrote a the.

Prong

It's best be humble
Before skewering occurs

On any brain-prong of our own
Polarities. Be humble not

(I hasten to adjust the claim) because
Of god, by god, whose names need no

Inserted caps nor yet
Inverted commas if you are

By nature skeptical about
The licenses and niceties. (Absurd

We should approach the heavens
With a yardstick. Arguments are ever

Fatally in love with punctuation. Hell,
I cotton to a semicolon now

And then myself, but not
To parse an *ars*.) Best just

Be humble since we can't
Tell much apart, the root

Of criticism from the
Flower, or the names

From someone's numb-struck
Nuncios. Of course,

I could be wrong.
(A single listener still

Could love the song.)

Missing Glove

I

A glance is a blow—
a force you feel—
or feel he feels, the more
your car obtrudes into

his lit proximity—the one
arm's-length of curb between
these traffic cataracts
contrarily aflow, now
slowing to a crawl, to a pause
of purring steel. They bring
the likes of you

then face-to-face
with the likes
of him.

II

Perhaps you fear
that forwardness of his,
and that unarmored gaze, his own
near-ominous
near-odious
near intimacy.

III

With a touch you make
your door secure—
an all-but-in-

offensive click.
What now, with all this
naked stretch of red light

set against us? Set about
your pantomime—the one
in which you cannot find,

at length, in the
glove compartment,
something you are missing.

IV

Needless to say there hasn't
been a glove in there
since nineteen thirty-five—

you can be sure the light will change
before a fucking glove appears!
A shrug might work. ("We only

came out for a ride!") Or how about
a sing-along? To tell the fella
that we care. "We will not stay,

we will not stare. We wish to
spare the ones who plead.
We know that you

would rather never
be regarded
in such need."

V

Look up, and you see red.
Look left and you behold
him holding up his sign.

Look right, so no one notices
he's touched your
handle, turned

your head.

VI

You turn your head and then you find
the feeling's everywhere. It's in the guilty-
looking truck, it's in the passing of the passerby,
it woos a woman from her break, unmans mechanics
at the shop, besets the tourists on their rounds, and snares
the sonneteer. No matter what we do, the world

is here; it's where we're stuck. For shame
or mercy, dark or bright, it means to find
a way inside. You've closed
your mind, you can't do more:
You can't get out

of sight.

Lament of the Touched

Detachment's being
thought achievable

is boggling in itself. Its being thought
achievable by love, a love
for all (not only every)
sentience (humankind and
animal alike), at times appears
the precept of

intelligences terribly untouched.
How much of a hand in things
must we have, to relinquish
the thing at hand?
What kiss of mind could such
communal sense permit? A swirl of dust
in theory perhaps? A drift of fish
in schools? Slow learners of
my sort must spurn

the selving sensualities, to feel
for feelers of this kind:
unfasten passion's
burners to discern

whatever's cooler under it.
In short, must court

dispassion just
to be compassionate.

From Sea to Sea

for Dot and Harlan Gardner, and the many families of Kiri

1. Humptulips Once Loved Meddybemps

Then Meddybemps became
A cleanup site. The past appeals
Until it just appalls; the trail
A way, a cause. But where we humans go
A curse recurs. Port Gamble's still

A little tinglish
From the rained-on
Revved-up power saws.
Its evergreening history's adored
As fiercely as Machias's; it cuts
To cultivate. A few of us

Continue pinging
Forthwest and anon
On our arcane affinities.
(In vain, at times: in English.)
No quirks of archaism cramp
The lumpy meter of the limpet's style;
The whales wail sensitively
From their amplitudes.

One local rag (its content
Lumberjacketed,
Disdained by droves
Of citybro on break)
Is where the border's
Latest weapons, new wave frequencies,
Are aired. (Should anyone
Be listening: The capitals
Are deafened by
Securitizing prose.
The ledger's tilted
Sharply on the ledge.
It gives a fart about the tender
In the sway.) One hardly knows

The cautionary from conclusive, among signs,

As now, from sea to sea,
First fiercely, then afar,

The starfish feel their feelers melt away.

2. A Bay Is a Sound

The fish have subtler schools
Than ours, and do not mull about

A border's Do Not Enter signs.
The strictest cedar stands for none

Of this "My-air-your-water"
Disputatiousness (though we

Have fed our toxins through the tree,
Whose systems so resemble those

Of human nerve). No matter
From what quarries, into air, the marks

Of capitals and shares and pseudo-
Independences be piled (to keep

Some reassured, and some reviled),
We find ourselves more naturally drawn

To one small child, whose wildest
Currencies we didn't know to seek.

She cannot talk. But she bespeaks
The raison d'être of a whole community:

Her neurochemistries are altered
Ampersands. She cannot dance;

She's curled into her chair. But let her see
The smallest light? She'll fill the world with radiance.

Fulsome's Not Wholesome

Handsome's a handful
And winsome's not bold.
Fulsome's past ample
(Toward awful, I'm told).

The fearful and fearsome
And quarrelful fall
Under finer command
When a man can recall

How the comely's not all
It is cracked up to be. And so

What if she's homely? She's wholesome
And partful! No more could be true.

(And no less could be artful.)

Category Error

———————

It's time to go to bed. Like it or
lump it, my brother loved to say. (That lump
contained a threat. Far harder than embracing relatives

is treating them with the respect of adequate
remove, as relatives in some
adventure never close enough

to breed familiarity. For every
one of us is strange.)
We err in having

too much time to bear, without
resorting to a zoom, descending
to a delve, or changing time markings

ourselves—then calling it a change in all
eternity. (The rate will always have a ticker in it,
and the speed of light an eye. We're blind

to our own frames.)

———————

And equally we err in having
far too little time to leave
the instances unlumped.

Each errs (what's more)
in her self-styling:
One in a million means

too many things. Two things, to start.
And one of those is self-aggrandizing:
The virtuous may say

I do. (One does believe one does.
But then belief confounds its wishes with
its will. As ever, instances

are odd. And odds are
it is evening.) Perhaps we rhyme
because we breathe.

———————

Out of a wet sack, into chilling airs
and hands of thumping analysts you're then
held close to the whisperings of one big fan—

your very own post-peristaltic, over-supervising mom,
first felt then followed, favored among all
the wet world's welter of

exterior decor. By now she's spent
so many months you can't
imagine, just to make

this possible, this minute
musical; to make you better
fed and fondled, regular and good. It's she

who tunes your living alternator,
feeds your focus, mum to mime,
a winking, blinking

cyclops in the treetops. You
were no one until
someone wild

got into her; then you were two
in one (as she was once,
upon a time). We all turn time

and time again. It's
knowable. It's true.
We breathe because we rhyme.

Unlumped

for Jonathan and Elliot, with fellow feeling

May I please be excused
from Irish class? If my identity
is going to be a group, may I
quit Group? I'd rather not be

swept along, or have to pay
a rubber-stamping coach for my most recent
forms of independence. Some are born
for war, perhaps, its corporals and

privates; others for a song: Love fucks
its chosen singletons, while hate
fucks states. (Some fuck it all. If I must be
swept up, well, please, then

make it only by
a breeze or broom—the stuff
of trees, whose beauty lies
in their distinction from

their families: a little
twist of difference, the secret name,
or signature incomparable, to be
their singularity.) There's not, on my ID, one thing

to make me different from the relatively bloodless
body they will find it on. And you can have
my father's brand, which marked my mother;
take her father's too, unpair the parent lines. I'd set

their instants free from instance, and their land
from ire. Let each one be
a passing circumstance, not
permanence's liability. Why do away

with everybody's better birthright?
Every homegrown boy or global girl,
each baby born urbane or
rural, starts off idio-

syncratic, homo-
sapient. Amen!
(Amen itself, o gods of war,
is neither negative nor plural.)

Stick

*for Jean-Baptiste Lully, inventor of the conductor's
baton, who died in 1687 of gangrene after stabbing
himself with his invention—in the toe—during the* Te Deum

Writ large, your knack for instrumental lilt
Became a squinting orchestra's anointer.
Beyond the sense of omen in your tilt
We owe you extra-dearly for the pointer.

Conducting every calling into air
You aimed for higher places, and you put
The emphasis on eye as well as ear.

High-handedness is what
The mass holds dear, but poets love

Your sacrificial foot.

Epithalamium

for Wynia and Ben

The wisest matchmaker would bring
Each mild, well-tempered country boy to greet
Such urban-girl combustibility. He'd sing
His heart out at the sight. She'd meet

His gaze without embarrassment;
She'd feather him in feelings past the norm
And bid him quit his country tent
To make a nest inside her dorm.

Still, caution's recommended for the groom:
From marriage's array of breast and thigh,
O rooster, after reveries of swoon,
Be careful not to cast a roving eye.

The peaceful farm can turn embattled ghetto.
Chicks command an army in a glance.
If on the road you would not sing falsetto,
You better keep your pecker in your pants.

What's Many and What's Big?

The winds are four. The seas
And continents are counted more,
By ordinary lights. (It's one to me.)
Immortal Newton (Isaac, not the fig)

Was pressured by authorities to keep
The count of rainbow colors down
To western music's scale. How odd!
(How *infra dig!*) Would covenants

Of god be made in only
Diatonic lights? Intone the sevens
When they could have twelves?
Are heavens so exclusive as to take

A shine to only customary seas?
Smile only on the couples
Who divide and not
The ones who multiply themselves?

Down to It

My passion didn't matter
To a soul, and all
My craving passion in return

Was one unholy imposition.
(I'm not saying holiness was on
My bucket list.

But couldn't I just settle
For a decent
Unarousability?) One day

I'd have to, when cremaindered out
On thickish air, resign myself
To a condition in which all

The coarse distinctions
(One or many, mineral
Or vegetable) become no more

Than taxonomic dust upon
An incidental breeze.
Was it not joy enough to feed

The plants, and mingle with
Some unchained dogs? THEY loved me
After all, with utter and unutterable

Loyalty. And after that, why ask a man
(And not just any man) to give up
All his high grammatical ideas,

Without a crampon or
A gulp of airlessness—and get
Right down to business,

Down to earth,
On such a muddy
Matterhorn as me?

Everybody Has a Fatal Disease

*

In the night, while it's quiet, I run
some lips across its ribs, some eyeteeth over
knucklebones, some mind downspine.

*

The saddest dog alive could still feel love. If you must
feel a feeling, that one's fine. And if you want,
there's a refinement: feeling transitive.

*

How comfort one another,
entre nous,
and never smother.

*

Animals feel love, and then
a want is born. To feel the want
can lead to wanting feels. Some kind

of blind comparative. Comparative
of kind. (Forget superlative, that
cloying fiction: it's the index

we are always
losing touches with,
and wasting touches on.)

*

For life, o life! The time-honored
condition. (Has living any
precondition?

Is it any?)
Moments aren't
repeatable. But do endure.

*

May I take
pictures of

your poor, afflicted
pelt? I am a well-

meaning American.

*

Life/death:
are you insured?

It's mutual.

*

From what is hard
to parse, or to control, or be
unimplicated by,

instinctively the lookers
turn their eyes.
The blind man has more sense.

*

The terror in the mirror tells
of being watched. The first gaze ever met was made
a double present of. A self's a sort

of obstacle to vision.

*

Absurd? You hear?

*

To feel
(for one's own
self) one feels out
others. But with
different feelers now.
We once felt smothered, so

we have become the smotherers.

It is the counterpart of
daddy's war. This time
this is THE life, we swear.
(But life's a mother.)

*

Of predicaments it is
the father, too. (The DNA of

the indictment: every creature
choked with feeling.)

Life the law, the Logos.
Uncommuted! Life

the sentence.

*

Come
to grips!
Look here. Look

here! or else

I cannot read your lips.

Intrans

. . . is of the slightest bondage made aware.
ROBERT FROST

*

Material for mezzo-masochist: Iron lady
Of the hot bath. Frigging object, banal item

All the awfuller for being so
Intoxicating, unsuspectable

Of motive. Rules (from here on in)
Are everything: You open up the tap marked C

And you have cheated. What's the object? Something
Cast for keeping heat, and capable of making flesh

Completely immunized against
The upstairs arguments (the voices rising,

Someone's M&D). You inch, you wrench,
You micro-meter in, toe, sole, then whole

Immeasurable foot, the curve of calf, which reddens
All the customary gold away, you hurt

All over, by degrees: the labia, the navel,
Nipples, bit by bit, you pry an angle

Toward the nape you hope
To drown in deafening. You don't yet have

A book to throw, but chapter, yes, and
Towel; you surrender. Verse for your

Aversions. Mine as well!
Since Prospero's are

Spells to be
Immersed.

*

Her mother bade her go. Her father
Went to war, or work, or some

Ellipsis. Then there were
Mediators. Doctors

Who would come to be
Her mother's form of faith.

Like Dr. X whom she engaged to fix
The legacy of overbite. He had a way

Of crooning to her, had
(He sang) to put

Her daughter under. Mum
(Who got her name from some

Of her responses) stood to kow and tow.
(Was it the title or the uniform? A dream

Of objectivity about the man?) Don't bother
To return till 6, he hummed.

(She didn't know
The nurses all

Went home at 4.)

*

One blinked one's looking open
In a dead-black room. Hot silvers

Tracked one's cheek. The patient woke, he said,
Up weeping. (Traces had

Been wiped away by someone's
Digits, or a dark dispassion.)

98.6, he said: Gal's fine. She only
Seems to have begun

(Today of all the days)
Her period.

*

One's mother didn't
Seem surprised.
Endure ordure,
All timbers, shivered,
Have a timbre. Take it to

Heart: of misery and of
Necessity a music can be made.
"Pickup at 6," he sang, and went
To cloak, to clock, to climb, to suscitate.

*

One cannot drown
Enough. Can't drown

The bounds of even one
Too-smarting self: the drink

One's in, the dream one
Flops across, the feeling quite

Firewatered out, the doubt
The phoenix swills about

The burning bush, and then
The pebble of a trouble (stubble

Cropping up to keep
A finger from its longer

Languorous intent.)
One cannot

Drown enough. One may yet need
Another object, in the deepening

Displacement.

*

Coming to,
One rushes toward

The multipliers. Multipliers, instruments
Of yawning, open wide. (Therein incisors

Wait, intently coupled up
For Caesar's argument.) One pays

One's dues, one dots one's dottables.
One comes to be a multiplier, too.

*

And there, of course, dementia lies,
Never so sure as in the finicking:

How small one was, or where,
Among the universes, moons;

Among the stars and galaxies, one
Planetelle emerging now to

Manage the emergency. O
Double down. You've worked

*

So hard, they say. Here's your
Reward, this stretch of the
Imagination. It's a headrest.

Now one needs no
Sentences. One needs no
Hands. Just lean upon

This pillowslip, let heavens whip
The mind, the flag, the wind, the
Words . . . In time they do

Not flag at all, they just
Wind down, and then
Mind not, nor even

Move. The nouns
No longer pounding things.
The verbs no longer

Taking bloody objects.

Post-Modernist Full Stop

Sun-showered mockery of cheer,
Sap-happy single face atop

A desiccated stalk,
Deserving admiration only

As an extra in a cast
Of thousands, where the kilo-

Meters can
Extenuate the scene

And dim the hubris of
The individual. A man

Could lose himself beneath
A thousand of his own ignorers, not unlike

Semblables, those adorers of
His self-ideal and

Overbearing trope.
O Sun God, God of Ones, you're

Foiled by astrophysics—unless time
Is our mistake, and one

Can magically reclaim
A former fast-eroding

Second personhood. Perhaps one could!
(The pronoun slips us, as it cannot

Slip the French! Ha-ha. Some gypsy hints
Toward a philosophy.) Each

Self-importance is a stand-in for
A species, and each species for its patch

Of interplanetary standing. Every
Planet for its polyverse. A period

Is no big thing, if you are headed
For the longer view, or just

Embedded in ellipses.

I Keep a Copy, Just in Case

I

My semiotics are undone by Ambien.
The airs are not reliable.
I find my meaning stymied through
the signage I'm
addicted to.

II

This film has language.

Earthlings raised
their flattened flags
upon its premises.
The moon could then proceed
to make them pure. Apostrophes
fell off. Coordinates increasingly precise,
the map grew dreamless.

Tell me when the homeland is secure.

III

My problems, or its problems, seem to be
a matter now of math, and now
taxonomy.
                The confident authorities

consign us to our stations, feed us
bird's-eye views and keep us
reckoned, ordinal from cardinal.
Let's dwell on this,

o votaries unversed in all
but universals: Commonest
of street names in America
is Second. Second commonest

is Third. And only third is First.

Two Exercises

1. A Sad Midlife's Base Report
*first line is from Yeats's "A Dream of a Blessed
Spirit"; title is an anagram of that title*

All the heavy days are over—
Now the fire-folk take the strand.
Brevities of night discover
Strokes in star-stream, laps in land.

From the east he came to learn
A sort of home, a port of time.
The hand upon Orion turns
A sword to anagram, the ring to rhyme.

With lofted mute and fluted grave,
One music can outshine a score—
Or incarnation be depraved.
The metronome the count adores

Can get no purchase on the heart.
The breakers stand to be appalled
By brokers; sea's most lowly part
Is just as inexhaustible as all.

And closely-held (as loves behave)
Became her—turning (fling on fling,
In Songhees strokes) to wave on wave.
The kindly universe of things

Which intellect inclines to mourn
Is there in one, one understands.
The humbled prospect's unforlorn:
The star is steadied by a hand.

2. The Twentieth Century and After

first line taken from Yeats's "The Nineteenth Century and After" (the key phrase of which—"the great song"— returns a few more times, in boldface anagrams)

Though **the great song** return no more
In air or folio, we're less
Demanding of it, in our
Anger ghettos. (**Agent got hers**,

Then got rages.) Meterless?
Get thee electron metronomes. No flow
Of cursives in your quill? Get Arial.
Throw in a few relaxatives for happiness.

Go gather tens, if hundreds wilt:
All manner of demeanings are in store.
In stock, in fact. In home decor.
(To love it IS to list it: beds atilt

Toward the Candy Cam.) But when
Her **anger gets hot**, **gags the tenor**,
Let the endless yesteryears be done:
Because for all eternity—and on

No more than enemas and anagrams—
Tomorrow's tiny tickers run.

As Authors Can't Perfect One Agent

an anagrammatical bagatelle: a line-by-line transliteration of Shakespeare's Sonnet 23

. . . so e-agents can't perfect an author.
His art (howbeit swapped shut) is his fire—
O high truth! A gloom-free writ! Some centerpiece
Whose hint (torn watchband) reawakens hugenesses.

Stuff for oratories? Go after toys.
Refer thy competence to lovers? Fie!
I neglect no minded systems, nor wave one hat.
(Wired for e-thought, two moving hemlines branch:

Queen bee, yokel tool. Both scent hem.)
Best pass as underbred, my king of rampage.
Download Homer. Look for pen of clever apes.
(Heather-thoughts: Hot art department! No more exams!)

Twitter HELLO earthward, to vanish alone.
Fetish's vow is now to be: All heterogeneity.

More and More

We're losing that distinction,
more and more, between
number and amount, between count
and size. There's almost

no such thing
as serious disinterest now—
there's just indifference. But WTF.
However many singers drink,

the fifth is undiminished. No less spirit,
only fewer spirits. Fewer characters—
but no less character. (We ain't got souls,
these days, but we got soul.) The day's

a tickered business.
It's our tricky destiny:
shaper of shimmers, on edges
of which, a half-inch down, clams hide

like gold in bread. Just playing hard to get.
A number's flashing into dusk, compulsive
lightning bug. The fractals mind
their subbranches. In our

proliferations of opinion we
are billionaires, our time ground down
too fine for any gear to have conceived—
you blink, and suddenly

a lustrum's gone. The stars are gotten up
in new electron microsequins—everybody wants
the eyeglasses that catch the fire—the race is on—
the race is on, my son, for more and more cheap

magical effects. Automatons can make it,
and a drone deliver it. And, yes, sir, that's
your baby, that's the one you bought
on time. Your dream has come with semen

pre-homogenized—who needs
Neanderthal romance? Cathect! Cathect!
With all these blinking lights, the old-time moon's
too hard to see—that amateur from way back when

a body needed to reflect.

Bad Dream, with Muzak

A gleaming plaza keeps its seven edifices
constantly attuned to Commerce Central.
Each appears untouched by any
shadow of a doubt.

Through overbearing portals,
high and low, on errands,
with their super-subtle humming
and their calm dispatch, some six and twenty

state-of-the-art Smart
Personal Flying Devices keep on
minding everybody's business. Under their drone
of cool efficiencies, among the statues in the square,

I am a mess: the only human there
without a PFD, without a ghosted
chance. Dull-footed, lacking glitterwork,
I scurry yon and near, from dark to

dark. At least the statues throw
more shade than glances. Still the shade
is minimal. The most prestigious of
the government departments is the ICU

where Interspecies Clean-Up can be
headquartered and motherboarded. (Friends
have wandered there, in hopes of mercy,
if not of repair. I've no such dreams.)

The hazard of my presence, my peculiarity, remains
entirely unremarked: these worker bees
are temporarily distracted, tending their
assembly lines, which soon

will pour forth Immortalities,
perfected finally. Though I'm unfixable,
and feverish, and fat, a splat
of Generation H, at least I'm still

beneath the notice of the zoomers.
(Twenty-six is nowhere near enough.)
It's all a matter of time.
(And heaven knows what hardware,

in what passes for a mind,
is keeping that.)

Galactic Politics

Aren't we yet
old enough? Have we not
called a truce? Or must we keep on

whipping every starfield redder
with our stripes? Our adolescence
surely should have ended

back in year 2008—if not
in '92, or '67. Hell, not even
Heaven, where we wave

our colors, seems to
set us right, although
upon our planet's

trademarked moon it made
the US flags we planted
all turn white.

Shape Up, Says Doctor Death

thanks to NBP, and after Blaga Dimitrova

Who's sicker? Someone saying
Just the one thing, over and over,
Or the one who runs from repetition,
As from conscience?

The man who lost himself—is he
The most afflicted? Or the man who's always
Seeking second selves,
The realer ones?

Can't you recall your name?
Or do you go around
Reminding people of it? Which
Is sicker? Come on, now,

Red-blooded health—
Let's take a breath,
Let's fill that chest!
What's this

Small chime I'm hearing
Near the ticker?—bit of broken
Nerve? A spot of bad self-pity? Bloody
Wheezing in the deep? Enough of that!

It's time to study
What the dying do.
They sob to laugh.
They sing to weep.

Breather

One wants to say to the dead
Come back this minute, you
Would love this new

Millennium, these next
Few lifetimes, even just an hour of ours!
But ah, there's never only one, one

Fails to say, except by dint
Of error; even the goose
Can gather more

Than two alone can celebrate, in
Honking alphabets.
And one may love

Specifically that errant one, fourth from
The end—o senses!—wherebefore all things
Are possible, wheresoafter

Only signs. What's come between us,
Mirror with your ever-loving
Doppelgang? What infant's crawled today

Behind the glass's ploy, to play
The flats and sharps we're always only
Telling of? I watch, intransitive.

That is the skeptic's motto. (Even clarity's
Delusory, unlike the sense of love, from which
Come charity and faith—and maybe even

Hope—though hope is hard, and faith
Is bodiless. We've ironized too long,
Shed rusty glances over every landing, every

Leaving season. Living still, we have
Our moments—one in a shine ignited,
One in a shout extinguished! Marriages of words

Remarking something measureless, as figures
Of affinity go listing down the rift.) Dear God, get
Down with us! Come back to be

In danger once again, and bear
The living gift—the giving in and giving out
That cannot be distinguished.

Responsorial

1. The Founder Animal

Once I was generated (for
about a million bucks),
I lay in their cage. I had

a transgenetic ID card.
I had no children and
I had no wife. I was what men

were coming to. I starred
in monitors, I uttered
asterisks. This was

The Life.

2. Old School

If the matter were solo,
No co- in the -cide,
You would merely be
(Meltingly)
Self-satisfied.

But the song calls for duo
(If not for a choir); nobody can
Wing it or swing it alone.
To your flightwork of flute
Came the lively pursuit

And to that came the
Higher and humming reply:
That whoever was giving
Or thumbing the ride,
And no matter to where

All were headed, or why—
You'd discover that you
Had a place in the new
(With a homey or two
By your side).

Some Sums

I

The rules are tricky, with the nuns.
I AM is both the last name and the first.
The middle name is THAT. That THAT
Is relative.

II

Then there's arithmetic.
The one and one and one
That don't make three.
(If we give Mom her due

III

There'd be another person of
Divinity, the grammar of its drama.
Hail the Holy Ghost. I love him most.)
Dad, so as not to die, wants Junior

IV

Sacrificed. It's downright Greek.
Little souvlaki, who made thee?
Some of the sums require
Component individuals

V

Be ushered into one big cattle car of the
Conceivable Totality, while others find
In every oddball several
Fallen eights. A number of

VI

Infinities. What manyness is man.
(A woman can contain what she will be
Contained by, so they say.)
The his-and-her denominations

VII

Hammer numbers to a door, in the name
Of names, in the battle of the Sum,
The conquest of the Some, the history of All
The Summiteers. In short

VIII

We find our parts
Forever streaming through
Some wholes, which all
Go streaming through the other

IX

Parts they are
A party to . . . et cetera. It's one
Big Being-fest, or Seeming-swirl,
A poker night the mind keeps

X

Trying to maintain
A hand in, but can never get
Ahead of (or, for that matter,
A bellyful). At least some God

XI

(The Author, possibly)
Has got a sense of humor—
Even as Another (let's say
God the Reader) weeps.

Old Gold

They take the ambiguity
for surety, the irony
for easy gems. The misanthrope's
"Good fences make,"
the killer's "eye sees not
itself but by reflection," and the bed
(the second-best) so famously bequeathed—all these

are bruited about, in moralizing tones, by elegiacal
clock-stopping doves and cops. "I thought that love
would last forever: I was wrong" is reconceived
as part and parcel of a mourner's lot. (It takes a mourner

oh about a flash, to see
the reading's insecure; and Frost, with all
his fencing, wouldn't turn out so
convivial; all that.) All through, it seems

the case was hopeless: latch
rustoleum'd until it could not open,
depths of discontent.
Or CONtent. Stress. Who cares.
There's nothing in it

for us, said the bureau chief.
(Mistaking irony for gems,
the other women get my husband's
praises, and his verse. I get what's far

more valuable these days: his teeth.)

Shots in the ICU

The unwritten CDs have stripes
of spectrum down their faces, there in their
transparent cases—perfect traces of
what otherwise would only be
a metaphor, or
gist, of history, instead
of light. The pure appearance

of refraction in these lines
can shift into the vertical; and that
is utterly resistant to
the daily laterals and dull
collaterals: its otherworldliness
the wilder for a fine precision slide: a close-up rainbow
several millimeters wide, a dwelling place
for uncontainables in analytic radiance to run
from the outer edge of a disc straight inward
toward its center, not in coils (the kind
that were concentric on his old LPs),
but deepening in radii from
two to three toward four

dimensions. His own bifocals
off for good, his hopes extinguished,
Dad keeps hissing, life's a swindle.
Birthing room to deathbed, that's
the line—a legacy from sunlight,
long profession now inclined
to sharpness, as the readouts turn
to shout-outs, shivers to Intensive Care's
own nursing station. There's the backed-up

window-ledge—no matter what the pandemonia, I'm going
to rest my sights upon that plumb line down
the centers of the stacked CDs, unreadable until

a setting star,
our own, brings out
a sense for it in me, lo and
behold! the rods and cones ferociously
inform the living hole with all
the spiked or spindled
evidence we need. O lazy pupil!
Crazy cornucopia! For I was blind
and you were blind

but now we have myopia.

To Be Expected

How generous can comprehending be?
And all of it the outgrowth of
an infantile blind grip (that meathook

mothers suffer from, and then
without: they have their own clasps
to undo). I've felt four times

the awesome, awful clawing from
the bed of mortal matter's state: two friends,
two ancestors. Each held out from the deathbed

one thin hand. That hand held on so hard
it hurt my own. But all it wanted was
for both of us to stay.

I pried our hands apart.
I slipped away. So they
Did too. And when

it came my time to say (of love,
for love, and to my living love) how
terrible those grasps had been—

what strengths the dying mustered on
their final day; how literal their grip had been
on life; and who was failing, who

betrayed—he
(ever undemonstrative) replied:
That's a cliché.

King Solomon's Marbles

What does a woman want?
SIGMUND FREUD

I

You lose them in your own excess
of rational negotiation: lose them
in an effort to stay fair, or lose them when you've paid
too much to the ax grinder (sharpener of blades, blunter

of women). Lose them trying to
find them. Agate suddenly ajar.

II

Right from the first, the curse
of being made (not born)

a king. (For kings are made by death—indeed
by many deaths: the right ones
have to go before you.)
Time is after all the feel

of fabrics of events. In you it flows
a little purple.

III

Even space appears
eventual. And so that all before you can
participate in presence, some
come after you: a vastness

constantly composed, and recomposed,
in particles of waves, in miles
of shimmering minutiae. You try
to line things up. You are beholden

to the lineage, as surely as the afterlife of laws.
(The lust is just sensational;
the love more purely
intellectual—perhaps more fool

than feel. With 700 wives, 300 concubines,
how wise can one man be? Unless
they shape him up.) In numbers,
people clamor after you, as people never did

before, more people, yellowing in papers,
deepening in beds, apportioning the blues, emoting
you to shreds. You see their eyes and seek
to satisfy—is this the standard? Is this

someone's sweet democracy? Your hide
was not well-hid, your kind not sparing, to

another's mind, when you,
so lordly, got to choose.

IV

So—on with it, decider! Out with it,
off with it! Remember the divine
example (one must kill to save
the kid). Let's see your

shiner, or your shooter, or your
killer of a regal kiss! You owed us.
Not just from day one, but also later,
when you cared to split

the difference: that single kid
was freeable, for once, from all
possession. You, by contrast?
Just a king, whose

immortality derived
from what his women did.

Underling

I offered to serve it, to make it
my lord. (And I took it for tall,
from the blips of report.)

But I've grown up since then:
All its *hauteurs* are fake.
Not for nothing those lifts
in its wingtips:

Time's short.

Moving Pictures: Post-Nup

1. Backed by Silver

I could make the man
Unwavering—if not in his regard,
In mine. To mind could call
His modeled moments:

Quicker fleshes,
Clearer clay.
Harder to see, to find
The armature or framework for

(The fashioner of fasteners)
Is me. I can forgive
The crook her veering, and the saint
His staff, the dead their downright

Out-of-sightedness: there's still
A them in it, for me. But to an eye
I say can see, how could
I look? How may I lie?

2. One Too Many

And it isn't you and they, but you and you
Who are estranged, whose own

Self-styling is the site
Of surfeit's cipher.

3. God Only Knows Where Women Keep Their Knives

Bulgarian proverb

"I fear this guy won't see me through,"
I wrote his mother, who was stuck back
In their native land.

I wondered if she deemed it true
A mama's boy grows up to be
A ladies' man.

I wondered if
A sea were just a sound.
I wondered if the right and left

Were interchangeable.
She nodded. That meant no.
It was a free country. The world

Was wide. So wide I couldn't
Wake up straight. Meanwhile,
He slept around.

4. The Mad Gardener's Husband

in collaboration with my ex

He thought he saw a spotted dick
Inclining toward the sky.

He looked again and found it was
A plate of humble pie.

(I haven't eaten out, he thought,
Since guzzling that K-Y.)

5. Ex-Wise

The stranger's not a station
Between strange and strangest.
Really it's ourselves, unknowable,

Ourselves we're most
Blindsided by. Coming through
The straightness of the rye,

A body meets a body from
So many decades back it makes
The insecurity express: You're

Un-alone, not one on the time-train,
Dreamboat, you once ten and now
Forever over. It was taller by half

And too large for the shelf.
Could he—or anybody—keep
Your hand in hand or thought in mind?

My means in names, I quite forget
Myself. What robbed the looker
Of her looks, the parent of

Transparency?
No mirror, just a living
Stream of frames.

Ex-Valentine

I had fallen in with lovers
—making love my raison d'être.
(There was quite enough rapacity in that.)

But now with Eros growing
threadbare and with lust
fast losing ground, I'd find

I could be free of airborne dust and its
combustibles at last, the rounds
of roadbed, battlefield, and furious

allegiances (which ape benevolence
but gobble up capacity, like ivy overcoming
oak). If you're intent on power—

if, devouring or devout, you're only
shooting to prevail—then go on
barreling toward Surefire

in your hail of hallelujas, but you'll do it
minus me. Get someone
gunger-ho or gunga-dinner

who can ride as sidekick in your pickup!
Someone fuller speed ahead.
My gear's reverse; my calling's

doubt; my idea of a curse
is certainty. Dearly departing,
with myself alone

I'll have my falling out.

The Catch

I

What year is this? What latitude?
I stepped into the centrifuge
and let it take the blame. BC
is somebody's SW; it has its share

of windmill palms. An orca climbs
a totem pole, a snowcap spews
hot ash. The psalms are undersung
in Mandarin, but sung at all

is something. Blessings follow
forefathers, gone forth
in legions, dead alone.
A warm front

screws the news up:
What once upon a time was letters
now is mangled into wording
on a weathervane.

II

And I remember the Southeast,
the towns where no one was allowed to say
"Well, I'll be damned." Where for the love of God
(or just so they could fight in peace)
my parents dropped us off at Sunday school.
The pewbacks straightened by a plated rule
had paper fans with ads on them,
for funerals and five & dimes.
The place was warm;
but wool's own worth
was soon reproving
rash behaviors,
in a Catholic uniform.

And then we moved.

III

And I remember the Northeast,
which styled itself with Manchesters and Belfasts.
Names were claims. And I became Aviva,
or Tamar. The towns put down a foot
and were not beautiful. Such
moralistic permafrosts!
Such ledges, hedges, and
inflations! What could grow in summer

grew; it snew from Halloween to Easter.
(Sou'westers were those rubber suits,
fish-hatcher's yellow, bellowing
above the blow.) A rooster
flew like mad above
the widow's walk.

IV

It wasn't till Des Moines I'd see
a manger that was not a prop on some dumb
county-courthouse lawn, a public nook
where animals on Christmas Eve

might be transported,
then were always
piping up unscripted, saying more
than preachers did. What did the preachers do,

who had to lose the likes of us
to Buddha-mind or (soon enough,
four decades on) to worse,
to Facebook?

In LA, angels

V

all wore leather, and our father
loved the border, or bordello (blue
Madonnas), while our mother boned up on
her Bloody Marys. Once rezoned,

resewn into our separable spaces, parts
were middle earth and parts were higher school:
the XY workaholic, and the XX homemaker—
they soon were left alone.

What shears or gears,
what Singer or Selectric could
improve a letter-muller's mood?
Myself, I couldn't wait to leave these

VI

states of mind—I thought I loved
the vinyl for its groove, believed I loved
the camera for its zoom. The grooms were dreamboats
even in the stills, were idling ably evermore . . .

And then we moved.

Little to Be

nor did I know
between bouts

(if an ear is a bout)
the pilgrim's pride

(out with it!)
dead giveaway

of thee I sing
who once applied

for the position
"loving brother

of every
lout" and land

on both feet
can be brushed off

each little one missed
and each big hit: all in

its arrow—not in store—
the happy band

along for the ride
on the roundabout to only

more and more
land where

my fathers died

Wandering at Night

for my brother and sister

God, a dog,
they say, big deal,
get over it, OK?
"Worse than a dog" is how
my drunken mother said my father,
all but dead in the hospice ward where she
knew better than to visit him, was being treated
by his kids. (Though all she knew of it was my
report each night before I crashed in the hotel.
That night I'd said we'd like
her help with the obituary.)

Really what she meant was
she felt like a dog herself—
he'd dumped her once upon a time and then,
when Wife the Second died, he came again
to ask her hand. As she was nine years younger, she
could see what that entailed. With righteous
indignation she said no.

And really what she meant was she
was terribly afraid of her own death, and his;
afraid as well that she'd become (in her
imagination of our own imaginations)
something to neglect. In fact
was sad for him, and for herself
who'd wound up left out, riddled
through and through with guilt,
unconsciously unkind.
The course of aging's

not a cruise, a friendly sky,
a warmer toddy: it's a grind.
Until it dies, a body loses sleep.
We're born to lose
the everything-in-mind
we meant to keep. But still I loved

the dog beyond—
as sensible accounts would say—
all reason. Poured into the vessel of
his patient bestial regard
my sediments of sentiment, my
heaviness of love. His belly hung
its weighted hammock from
the tentpoles of his hips; he groaned
when he lay down; and after two long seizures,
when he most required to sleep, we mercifully

arranged for him to die. O brothers, fathers,
sisters, mothers: One cannot seem to love

oneself, as such.

Only as others.

Between Beaver and Sappho

Clallam County, 2018

There's news here, too. It's everywhere.
The hell-bent men who went around
The bend. The women learning they must lie
Less quietly. Ingot

No one can trust, although the Hill's
Pretending to consider. Cannot sit
Or stand a bit, away or down, nor yet
Give out, without an upstart's

Cry and hue: No more! No less! But where
Were they, when you were dusting
All of Alexandria? The elephant in every
Room! (The donkey, too!) O history,

Take up your broom, and bless
This mess hall full of animals.

for Michael Lynch

Emerita

I'm winded now, and golly, how!
who started off as drafted.
I thought I got the thrust, but now
suspect that I was shafted.

I loved the well and loved as well
when winding sheets were new.
With anapests on every hand, I felt
my dactyls, through and through.

Who murdered all the annuals
while I survived my menses?
I was a sensualist and still
they took away my senses.

I was a carnival of thought;
I danced the spirits off their feet!
But look what public life has wrought:
now I'm an aesthete.

Picked Up at the 3-Way Intersection

I

When he was just a boy in Edinburgh
A. Graham Bell contrived

a talking doll. The doll said "Mama."
Later, it appears, he wouldn't ever

telephone his mother or his wife. (They both
were deaf.) These facts can make

a grown-up, all at once,
and all alone,

lie down and weep real tears.

II

The Himalayan, largest
of the honeybees, makes honey notable for its
hallucinogens.

(Hallucinogens for us, that is.
Of *their* imaginations, we

are ignorant.)

III

Do geese see god?
the dog-god asked.
The question and
the questioner himself

are perfect palindromes.

IV

Antarctic glacier ice
is known to test
as high as 3 percent
for penguin piss.

V

Within an average
human lifetime
you produce

saliva of a quantity
to fill two good-sized (if
completely uninviting)

swimming pools.

VI

Did you know oysters change
their genders as they will? It's not that they
are exhibitionists. Oh, no. At these
slow dances, they are only out

to multiply their chances.

VII

After a battle's lost, an ape
inclines to masturbate.

In this, as in
much else, he quite

resembles humans.
(Human *men*, I mean:

our women much prefer
to jack off when they win.)

VIII

Just off the coast of Iceland
climate-change researchers
were dredging earnestly
for clams, to check
their age and health and see
how global warming was affecting them.

They froze and then dissected
several hundred clams, which now
(quite unsurprisingly)
could qualify

as dead. Among
the gathered clams
they found this one

whose shell rings
placed its birth at five to seven
hundred years before. In other words,
they learned they'd killed

the oldest animal on earth.

IX

Perhaps for all these reasons
(if in formicultural domains
a reasoning endeavors to exist)

no ant
can sleep.

No ant is sleeping, ever.

Quid Pro

I

What's the neuter singular
of who. No question. Pound

is nothing, sound or fury, next
to Bond. Some bonds no wands

would want, like those that underlie
the instruments of reference

or those that underpin
the diapers on the dictator, the one who makes

a means assessable, but no
amends. He weighs the ways. He has

two hands. (Right hands, of course—because
the opposites attract, and heaven knows

he may not love a man.)

II

Your customs agents, fatherland, do mucho
potty-mouth and petty-coat on duty.

Meanwhile, underneath
your unsaid *Arbeiten* of gate

the unofficial peoples stream.
Each time the timer's touched,

it bends a little light: we can't remove the sight
from guns, our fingers from the sight. (A lid

is sixteen grams, the scales fall
up. All hands

on dex!) That's why the poet's
discontenting: nothing's

known by numbers. Let us do
a number now.

III

Et puis je fume! It all goes up
in mirrors, suddenly the stupider

securities are monetizable—the highest
of degrees, the cooked among

the books, the haute.
O art!—aye, there's

the rub!—it's rare, it's never clearly
done. The writing's writhing, all

the animals in etymologies
are spirited. The poets leap

in air (in error!) to escape
a living room—the room

of articles, the second story's
narrative. The sin is not

original: it's just as hackneyed
as inherent. Practice makes it—

yet it bears revealing: Every death's
the only death. (Again!

This time
with feeling.)

Newborns On Display in Boxes

Let's not get one of those.
Entirely unadjusted to the human hue,
They all are bald or bellowing, loud blue.

Not one is recognizing you
For the incomparability you are—
Each feels his sluggish way along

The reddest runneled bulges of
The hallways in his gut
And brain, to gain

A glimpse only by chance (one
Here, one there) of all
The brilliances attending him.

That one before you, for example—he's
A fist of physics, monkey business, uttermost
Interiority, and lest he soon forget it,

He'll be tested with a grippe, or clamp,
Or crapper latch they'll soon enough be telling him
He'd better manage. For the moment, though,

He scrunches up, he stretches out, he twists
The pivots off his looks, and flinches
Into aftershocks for days. Eventually a gaze

Emerges. (That's how selves—and persons,
More desirable by far—I speak as one
Lifelong grammarienne!—are always

Coming to exist. Not only he, incubatee, but all the
Other lusty brutes, like you, arrive: forever
Unfamiliar telegrams.) He opens up

Because a nipple pointedly
Addresses him, a lap enlists his
Second (subintendent) lip and then

Before you know it, he's becoming
Something altogether else—
Somebody someone

Can't resist.

Range

I

So much appears
unfit for poetry. To rage about

the insular, to croon about
the moon. Romances

of the narrow mind, instead of the widening study
of actual bedrock. Meanwhile

at school the rule
gets readjusted, that inevitable skit

updated out of laugh tracks into
advertising jokes. The heart cannot

go out, consigned to five
accessoried electives!

Nor mind.

II

Let's set the lot of them
to sea at seventeen, the kids

of everyone, to work
at wonder, somewhere all

their parents once thought
foreign. Send them off before

they're glazed, or glorified,
committed to the latest therapies or

moral ardors; before they're payable by year
or parsable by fashion. Let them float, or fly, or

somehow fathom something, literally
immersed. Not fret about what's fast, or first,

or fooled or failed—just get to be
amazed. Let's find them

one more chance at
curiosity instead of greed,

surprise in place of
a recliner, somewhere change

is not a lucre's
superfluity but life's own

streaming science. That's
where dreams are

unbespoke; where folks are
unfamiliar; and a range

is no appliance.

Post-Polymath

*in consideration of Frank O'Hara, whose poetry I never, in my
not-so-subtly stuck-up youth, could learn to love*

I'm healthier now that I take drugs,
can sleep, and every day eat more
than medical advisers recommend.
What then is health?

I don't have nightmares,
I don't sleepwalk, don't have fits
of all-night tightrope challenge, as of yore;
I don't twist hours over ticker-taxing deeps.

I'm not now fed the bad rice pudding
I so often kept in cheek
until I was excused, or else could sneak
to tuck into the houseplant's soil the moment

they were deep enough into their nightly
argument. I'm perfectly well-fed, and they
are dead. The dumps I was so down in,
after being dumped,

have ended—I don't need them back, or any
of my own and youthful greed, to please or just
excel (those drove me past all peace);
the obscure charms of thumping away on any

stranger's belly, being bumped up, bum in air,
or groan-anointed, nose in groin—what have you!—all of it
is sweetly lost on me these days. I come and go just as
I please, I love the other arts of nature, rest my way

out of the contest—let the fuckers win! And let me be
just comfortably numb, an airhead or a pothead, a statistic in
a zolpidemic, making myself nothing, all day long,
except (at length, at dusk perhaps,

in acts unauthorized
by maths, or *poésie*)
a good bright product
from a good dim sum.

The Truly Screaming Baby

Thank god says the woman in 13E
we're not back there. She means
back there with the mom
with the truly screaming baby
and two toddlers more, to boot,
who didn't once (my seatmate sourly now
informs me) in the pre-board waiting area obey
a word she said. The baby sounds
in agony. We haven't even yet entirely
taxied out to takeoff. Not one passenger
appears remotely sympathetic, so I can't help

wincing on the mom's behalf. What if
the baby's sick what if she's always
like this and the mother's feeling
permanently miserable since even
on this getaway she cannot get away
what is a flight if not an escapade and now
her fellow passengers are blaming her
for what she can't escape or even partially
ameliorate what if they're penniless and this
is her one chance to visit relatives what if the father's
always off carousing and comes home an hour or two
at most to get her pregnant once again then take
her just as much to task for noise as these
more pampered people on the airplane do
what anyway could make this baby's life so utterly
unbearable who has no words to say it better
here for us it's just a hundred twenty
minutes surely mom had never
dreamt of being famous to the world this way
nor when she planned a family imagined
she'd be here appeasing kids in pain or
terror or in god knows what unending
rage how can she possibly
contain the other two
how can they fail
to opportunize on
the baby-made commotion
sure enough a wail now rises from

the middle child a bid for mom's
attention in the fray must she remain
alive for all of them?

And really, what's this baby's
meaning, so convulsed? (I can't begin to say

how soul-wrenching the screaming is, as if a scalpel were inserted
deep within her ear—who chooses that?) Now kiddo #3
would like to share her own exploratory song but all along
the nightmare is the baby's, while the rest of us
are only irritated, disappointed, lonely,
wishing to be heard as much
as left alone. Life's awful,

we are slaves, if not
to parents then to poverty
or policy or pain, the grinding at the nerve,
the unexpected growth, or cavity, if not in others who
desire or who despise us, then in our desiring or despising,
under legacies of time and DNA and worse—these make us prey

to weepers, leapers, addicts, habits, wedding bells, or
verse. Yet given here the chance to fly
for once to someone's aid we all

sat grudgingly and didn't try.

Original

What was the gender
of the foot's original and rightful
owner, so to speak? One wonders

whose foot is it now, if only
legally. A foot alone
washed up. Where is

the rest? All rocks
in this vicinity.
Does this one left

match any of the five
right feet in this coast's
ever-more-macabre history?

Is every sixth a part of some
hellish hexameter? How much
of composition is the silent part. No

question. Not all poetry
is song. Each year the merry maid's
December'd, and the paragon of pure

congeniality becomes some less-
than-celebrated frumpiness.
Yet every girl was born to be

the one-and-only
model of her kind. And on behalf
of all those missing moms—

the ones they had,
or ones they could have been—
I pray the littlest of her

metatarsals be
hereafter and herewith
remembered.

There's Kind and Then There's Kind

in memoriam AWM

My friend felt every carnal suffering and spent
her lifetime nursing damaged animals.
Neurotic parrots liberated from the parrot shop,
the pigeons rescued from the hungers of the hawk,
the dogs delivered to her door. And some
had chains embedded in their necks
and some had recoil in their eyes. But all
of them, abandoned or abused, were given
new protective pens and household latitudes.
Coddled and kibbled, they lost
the habit of their suffering.

At large are live leviathans whose calm
communications can't compete with our
speed-stung technologies. They got the name of Right
because they floated when harpooned,
and so were harvestable. One of the most

unprepossessing flour beetles was
mistaken for another, so in taxonomic annals
it is called Confused. Another had a hollow in its back;
that was the one the beetle-men would dub Depressed.

And once my friend had been informed
her tumors would be Terminal,
her husband up and took
a trip to Paris, with a pal.

Some times will make you want
to burrow deep in some
obliterating bed. But we
leave tracks, or traces, trails.
And much of what we think or say
won't help. He held her later, when a lot
of others were away. What's right? What's

wrong? (What's diagnosable? What's healable?)
Today my friend is dead. But as she had
her last, and worst, and least
time-buying chemo, I remember
what she said (what none
of us who loved her could
so answerably claim):

"Now I've felt everything feelable."

L3FT R16HT

*in memory of Elena Popova, my mother-in-law,
back then*

One shoe
was on

the dead one's
foot and went

with her. The other
stayed on the third

step from the top,
and is there yet,

for those who aren't
entitled to forget.

The when and where would soon enough
be said and done. (A gown can be

a drag, for instance, given
the current events or the holes

in your craft. But she had moon-
and-stars pajamas. I've been assigned

to study everything since then.
Look floaters up. Get eiders down.

And tell some kind
of truth.) The last detail

in both her presences (the one, after the fall,
when she was still alive, irreparably alone;

and then the other, in which medical
examiners would stand too close to her

by-then-eternally averted gaze)
was some enormous particle, right

at the stairway's base—a bit
of dust I'd failed, first once

and then forever,
to sweep up.

For the Record

Compelled for all those years
to record what I saw,
what I felt, what I thought—
in all precision and intensity—

Did I have too much time? I think not.
Or I feel not.

Nowadays I cannot tell
the two apart: can't feel things thoughtlessly
or think things up without emotion. The world felt
endless to me then, perhaps, and needing
categories, angles, clear containers.
Stills and seizures, insights built
on glances, glimpses.
Later, glosses were applied.

But then your vitreous
detaches, first in one eye then
a few weeks later in the other:
flashes from a corner of your vision
settle into shorter threads
that float around in one
direction then
another, as if down

the slip-curve of the globe. Forever after that,

the world is slightly blurred; it's
mediated; it is not immediate.
And as for thought, well,
thought is not

the curve, and not
the gloss, and not the thread
or snippet. Certainly it isn't any
luster just behind the scenes,
obscene, inside
the seeing,
bothered by
the intervening

gauze, but eager
to ignite another
seer. No, no, the thought

can be forgone or, better yet,
forgiven, since
it does its best,
and loves its nothings.

(Nothing seems so clear.)

World View

Capitol Hill, Seattle

I

A horizontal stripe the length
of one whole city block
has blackened in a blink.

And now the next line up
blinks on. Some sixty windows make
the cinematic strip through which

so tinily and steadily that single figure
moves, fastidious in ceremonies near
the desk-lamped cubicles . . .

II

And recently retired, across the way,
I seem to have, by contrast, city leisures,
and my views on heaven. Haven't had
to lift a finger yet, since moving in, nor let

a damn shade down.
I'm looking out. This is my own
custodial responsibility, who cannot
count the ways I took to get here, along

shores and forests, breezes, shadows,
mushrooms, moons, and fox-cub generations
tumbling through the brushwork of the
tide pools where they played. Uncountable the stuff

of decades that I took for
granted, as the years eroded
down to rockpiles and began to grow
some cemeteries. Cities too, it seems, require

disinterested investment.
Like the other wildernesses, they instruct us
not to love the lions more
than poor hyena hangers-on; and not to prize

the heated vehemence above
the evenhanded cool. (Uh-oh. Do I detect

the fool for love again emerging,
nonetheless a fool

for time, a wariness of
symmetries? Why not?) Let's talk.
It seems that otherwise
we're stalked by only greed and fear,

through all our dear amusements and
abuses, taking out insurance for
a casualty, Viagra for a verve. Is everyone
as unintending to be cruel

as foxes on the prowl? That heavy
breathing that you hear is just
I-5, the interstate—a traffic in
the darkness, mercifully relieved

of makes and models, down to only
two broad brushstrokes, differentially
applied, of midnight's trades:
one way is silver eyeshot,

and the other is a scarlet wake.

III
Then, morning brings its multitudes again.
All memory's a tickered trick, confounding mind

with its reminders, and authorities with
editors. My god, my ignorance

could still be appetite's, my
meanings blind, my view

the predator's . . .

Long Enough

for Rich Hladky

*

Caught up in parallaxes of impure
proximity, attracted to the matterworks

of you, the swerves of heft
and heat my meathooks

must, by nature, twist to just
accommodate, however might

my kind resist? We have
to long, who look for love.

We long to look.

*

I love the hook. As long as five
mere senses of you can obscure

a half a billion planets,
I'll be powerless.

*

Eventually—if I were pried away by a big enough
lever, or demands of others, or a many-worded lord;

if I were lured by other minds, or room to roam, on Earth with
a capital letter, in Man's own manifestic universe;

by thoughts of one
sense only, or a thousand more

resistances to countlessness—could anything
again be cool, be clear

about the boundaries? If then
I saw a sea, so similarly using

ships for flash, or met another mountain
brandishing its stars, or when a new

Orion thrust his spear as hard and deep
into my one mind's eye, could I
be unreminded?
or so near re-blinded?

or so far asleep?

*

Just to be freed from greed,
just to be un-time-shared, must we
who can't be long around

forever live in hunger or in
coldest solitude? Suppose I dared
to set my sights upon

some über-grand, some ultra-hot
idea to come, to compensate!
Your vision being somehow as

ferocious as your venery, I fear
that even then, my love,
you'd spare me not

a lick of fate.

Descendant Song

*Your dead cease to love you. . . . Our dead
never forget the beautiful world.*
LEGENDARY WORDS OF CHIEF SEATHL

Our dead love the killer pods
still frequenting the islands.
K-pod's granny whale was born
in 19 and 11, same as your own dad

(and not too far from his
Nanaimo crib). But she went on
to well outlive him, though he lived
to 87. Your dead cease to love you

even while alive; they think of play as
way of life, fast-forward as imperative,
rewind as just a quaint old term
the techies in the sky need not replace.

There is no interceding with such gods.
Our children love a lot of things,
but mostly us, and where we live.
Your children love their iPods.

52-Blue

for Christopher Frizzelle

*

I cannot get enough of him
In quite a different sense from that

In which the others can't.
My senses endlessly seek out—

Or conjure up—his presences.
He calls like crazy to a heart.

Their way can never hear him,
Who is recognizable in waves

No other blues can understand.
And since their sounds are virtually

The way they see—and since the medium
On which they ride is such

A textured place—tormented more
Than ever now by

Gongs of commerce, overloads
Of tech (subsonic, ultrasonic,

Supersensible), the throngs of war, the threads
Of espion, and more—it's all that the

Community can do, to keep
In touch with one another,

Without translating for him,
The hapless 52.

*

And how can he—without
The flickerings of a community's

Affection, or familial alert (to danger, or
For food), without those wild-silvers of wavelength

That will twine all tones in touch and make
The magic of a species passion—how

Can anyone so long alone
Feel safe, or known, or loved?

Must he go on exploring all the shimmering
Cathedrals—kelps and corals—or the deeper

Promises of gloom, forever looking
For another like himself, in

Frequencies perennially
Uncorrected by exchange,

More wild and more inquiring at
Each submarine remove?

He turns the forests with his tail; he touches
Tunnels with his lip. And only rarely—

As if in a dream—he catches
Someone's odd, unfathomable

Glance: a drift of silver,
Gist of blue—a ghost or god

Whose partiality to him
Now flashes from

A mirrored room
Inside a sunken ship.

Stay Already

*

What day is it, this
Time? A Valentine's?

A gift of dreamy
Downfall, finally?

Or is it even yet
The present? (Is it still?)

Could it not settle for
Some plain-as-day

Identity, like Saturday,
Let's say? Must all

Forever be becoming? Never one
Conclusion we can call

Foregone, though soon is
Dying to be done.

*

A bind. What is it?
Valentine's? A same boat

To be in? The sixty-
Somethings every hour. Let's

Count! One thousand
One. One thousand two.

Time's up! (It's also down,
Toward now or

Never: flowing,
Flown.) It's damnably

Mistakable for
Space. We row

And rest. The craft's
A creature of its own.

The current's moving.

On the Fourth Day

with, and for, Rich Hladky

Suddenly everything
Stayed the same.

We who had called
The water blue

Refocused on our lenses. We
Who had seen the island move

Reunderstood our oars. The sand
Composed some drumlins in the sound

While we revised the sky. And whether we saw fog or not,
The sun still burned alive. Arose, along the tidelines,

Ever un-updated news. (Some news was not
Of men.) A day and a night were number five.

And suddenly nothing changed again.

About the Author

Heather McHugh frequents the Salish Sea areas of western Washington State and southern British Columbia. In addition to her 2009 MacArthur Fellowship, she has won many distinguished awards for writing and for teaching, having taught for decades at the University of Washington in Seattle as well as at the MFA Program for Writers at Warren Wilson College (and elsewhere). Between 1979 and 2009, collections of her essays, translations, and original poetry regularly appeared in print. *Muddy Matterhorn* is her first full-length collection in ten years.

Poetry is vital to language and living. Since 1972, Copper Canyon Press has published extraordinary poetry from around the world to engage the imaginations and intellects of readers, writers, booksellers, librarians, teachers, students, and donors.

WE ARE GRATEFUL FOR THE MAJOR SUPPORT PROVIDED BY:

THE PAUL G. ALLEN
FAMILY FOUNDATION

4
CULTURE

Anonymous
Jill Baker and Jeffrey Bishop
Anne and Geoffrey Barker
Donna and Matthew Bellew
John Branch
Diana Broze
John R. Cahill
The Beatrice R. and Joseph A. Coleman Foundation Inc.
The Currie Family Fund
Laurie and Oskar Eustis
Mimi Gardner Gates
Gull Industries Inc. on behalf of William True
The Trust of Warren A. Gummow
Carolyn and Robert Hedin
Bruce Kahn
Phil Kovacevich and Eric Wechsler
Lakeside Industries Inc.
on behalf of Jeanne Marie Lee

TO LEARN MORE ABOUT UNDERWRITING
COPPER CANYON PRESS TITLES,
PLEASE CALL 360-385-4925 EXT. 103

WE ARE GRATEFUL FOR THE MAJOR SUPPORT PROVIDED BY:

Maureen Lee and Mark Busto

Ellie Mathews and Carl Youngmann as The North Press

Petunia Charitable Fund and adviser Elizabeth Hebert

Gay Phinny

Suzie Rapp and Mark Hamilton

Adam and Lynn Rauch

Emily and Dan Raymond

Jill and Bill Ruckelshaus

Cynthia Sears

Kim and Jeff Seely

Randy and Joanie Woods

Barbara and Charles Wright

Caleb Young as C. Young Creative

The dedicated interns and faithful volunteers
of Copper Canyon Press

The Chinese character for poetry is made up of two parts:
"word" and "temple." It also serves as pressmark for
Copper Canyon Press.

The poems are set in Helvetica Now.
Book design and composition by Katy Homans.